FAITH LESSONS FOR LITTLE ONES: VOLUME 2

Copyright © 2024 by Spirit & Truth
All rights reserved.

Printed in the United States of America. No part of this book may be used or reproduced in any manner whatsoever without written permission except in the case of brief quotations embodied in critical articles or reviews.

For information contact:
SPIRIT & TRUTH
PO BOX 1737
MARTINSVILLE, IN 46151

spiritandtruthonline.org

Written by Renee Dugan
Illustrations and Cover design by Ghyvari Ben Medie
ISBN: 979-8-218-36927-9

First Edition: February 2024

10 9 8 7 6 5 4 3 2 1

Job
(The Book of Job)

There once was a man named Job who seemed like he had it all—wealth, family, friends, a very comfortable life! But then he lost it all when the Devil attacked him. Job's friends tried to pin the blame on Job's behavior, but Job stood up for himself and for God. He even got to speak to God and learn from Him! After that, God blessed Job with an even greater abundance than he had before. Job's faith in God never wavered, and he was rewarded greatly for it!

Abram becomes Abraham
(Genesis 12–25)

God called a man named Abram to go from his home country on a long journey to serve Him.
Abram was old and had no children, but he took his wife Sarai, their nephew Lot, and their households, and went. They faced a lot of danger along the way, but God proved Himself faithful everywhere they went. He even gave Abram and his wife a son! He changed their names from Abram to Abraham and Sarai to Sarah, and they named their son Isaac. God rewarded him greatly for his faithfulness.
He was even called "friend of God"!
Thank You, God, for always being faithful
and loving toward us!

Joshua
(The Book of Joshua)

Joshua was a brave, strong man who left the land of Egypt when God freed His people from the hard-hearted Pharoah. When God's prophet Moses finished leading God's people, Joshua took over. He and his friend Caleb helped God's people conquer Canaan, the land God promised to them. There were tall, scary giants and big cities full of cruel people trying to stop them, but Joshua served God and didn't let anything stand in his way. With his leadership, the people finally made their home in the land God promised to them!

Samson & Delilah
(Judges 13:–16)

For a long time, God's people didn't have a king ruling over them, they had judges who passed along God's judgement. One of them was named Samson. God told Samson to never cut his hair, and Samson obeyed: he grew up to be so strong, not even groups of his enemies could stop him!
He survived no matter who attacked him. But then he told the secret of his strength to Delilah, a woman he fell in love with, and she sold it to his enemies. They cut off his hair and captured him! But Samson prayed to God, Who brought his strength back one more time. Samson defeated more enemies that day than he had his whole life!

Thank You, God,
for giving us strength when we need it most!

Elijah & Elisha
(1&2 Kings)

God sent lots of men and women to speak to His people when they disobeyed Him. One man was named Elijah. Elijah prophesied while there was a King and Queen who were wicked and prayed to other gods, and even convinced God's people to do the same. Elijah helped wipe out people who were following false gods, but it was hard work and he was tired, so God brought a man named Elisha to take over. Then God moved Elijah somewhere in the world where he could live the rest of his life in peace. Meanwhile, Elisha continued Elijah's work, wiping out the people who worshipped false gods and helping bring God's people back to Him.

Thank You, God, for raising up people to help us remember we should always follow You!

Ruth & Boaz
(The Book of Ruth)

There was a woman named Ruth who married a man from Israel when his family came to stay in her country. When he died, Ruth went to live with his mom back in the country of God's people and help take care of her. Ruth started following God and worked in the fields of a man named Boaz. Boaz liked Ruth and wanted to marry her, but first he made sure no one in her old husband's family wanted to marry her. No one did, so Boaz asked Ruth to be his wife. She said yes, and it was a marriage that had God's blessing...they were part of His plan to fix the world!

Thank You, God, for providing for those who follow You!

King Solomon
(1 Kings: Proverbs)

God's people had a great king named Solomon. God asked Solomon what he wanted from Him, and Solomon said, "Wisdom!" So God made him the wisest person who ever lived. Solomon even wrote a whole book of wise sayings called Proverbs! He solved lots of arguments and built a big house for God, called the Temple, that stood for hundreds of years. Even though Solomon didn't always do the wise things he knew to do, especially when he got older and listened to advice from bad people, he still did a lot to help God's people.

Shadrach, Meshach, and Abednego
(Daniel 2)

Shadrach, Meshach, and Abednego were three of God's people living in a kingdom that was far away from God's Promised Land. The king of that foreign land had a dream of a huge statue, and he liked it so much he had a golden statue made and commanded everyone bow down in front of it. When Shadrach, Meshach, and Abednego refused to bow down, the king had them thrown into a very hot furnace as punishment. But God sent an angel who protected them in the furnace, and they weren't hurt! The king was amazed and started to worship God, and he promoted Shadrach, Meshach, and Abednego.

Daniel
(The Book of Daniel)

Daniel was one of God's people living in a faraway kingdom. He served God with all his heart, but some leaders in the kingdom hated him for it. So they tricked the King, who liked Daniel, into punishing him for worshipping God. The King was upset, but he followed his own law and put Daniel in a den full of hungry lions! But God protected Daniel, and in the morning the King found him safe. Daniel kept serving God, who sent angels to show him dreams about the future that are still important today!

Thank You, God,
for protecting Your people no matter where we are!

Queen Esther
(The Book of Esther)

Many of God's people lived in a kingdom whose King was looking for a new wife. From all the women, he chose Esther, one of God's people, to be Queen! But the King's advisor Haman was angry with Esther's cousin, Mordecai, and he wanted to wipe out all of God's people. Mordecai begged Esther to help, and even though it put her own life in danger, she approached the King for help. When the King found out Haman's plans, he was furious! He got rid of Haman and gave Haman's job to Mordecai. God's people were saved thanks to Esther's bravery.

The Disciples
(The Gospels: The New Testament)

God's Son, Jesus, didn't just come to save the world. He came to train others to save more lives after he was taken up into heaven to live with God. His first followers were called "disciples," and there were twelve of them he was really close with.

They learned from him and were empowered to do miracles like he did. One of the Twelve turned his back on Jesus for money, but the others stayed faithful. After Jesus left, they spread the good news about him even in very dangerous places, and he continued to inspire them just like he inspires us! Thank You, God, for empowering and inspiring us through Your Son, Jesus!

Apostle Paul
(Acts: The New Testament)

There were lots of people trying to stop the spread of the good news about Jesus, but one of the worst was a man named Saul. He attacked anyone who followed Jesus! But God had big plans for Saul. He sent Jesus to speak personally to Saul, and after being blind for a few days and healed by God's power, Saul's heart was changed. God changed his name to Paul and sent him on many dangerous but important missions to spread the Good News. Paul wrote lots of letters to teach and encourage people who follow Jesus, and they are still here to teach us today!

Thank You, God, for redeeming even the hardest hearts to serve You!

www.ingramcontent.com/pod-product-compliance
Lightning Source LLC
Chambersburg PA
CBHW061357010526
44107CB00012B/962